RIVERAIN

Riverain

ROBERT POWELL

VP

Valley Press

First published in 2018 by Valley Press
Woodend, The Crescent, Scarborough, YO11 2PW
www.valleypressuk.com

First edition, first printing (March 2018)

ISBN 978-1-912436-01-9
Cat. no. VP0121

Cover and text design by Jamie McGarry.
Cover photograph from the Susan Parr Collection.
Edited by Martha Sprackland.

Printed and bound in England by SRP Ltd, Exeter.

Supported using public funding by
ARTS COUNCIL
ENGLAND

LOTTERY FUNDED

Contents

for Dianne

and to river-watchers and river-keepers everywhere

riverain (ān)
(adj), of a river or its neighbourhood. (n.), riverside dweller.

Source

Not at the knowing coordinates
pinned down by rods
and chains, zenith telescope
Ramsden theodolite or US satellite
to triangulate the genesis
of writing or watercourse

but in this winter pool
on a farm track
glass tossed by wind
or the dream
of a child asleep
in a Saxon place-name

that slips among
roots from the lips
of a buried mother
ice-made, furled,
who waits for her people
to wake up, wake

to see the sky
walk on water
the depth of a salt tear
far from the sea
a welling jewel
riverseed

sown where thought
turns to words
that squirm in warm mud
and flow onto a page
open like a flood-field
here.

PART ONE

Appearances

Sleeping Under a Tree Among Horses

Unguarded in the branched dusk
they graze the buried roots
with their humble beauty
and old friends, the flies.
They've been here a long time,
know the place well, and pay you
no attention as you arrive,
which feels a kind of love.

All day and long before
you've been walking from battle
or hunger, or the common crime
of living and forgetting;
so beneath that summer oak
into which the day is draining,
on the grass sheared tight
by their patience, you lie down.

All night in that unexpected hospital
you sleep among them, huge nurses,
their shapes dark arcs under the stars.
At times you hear the rush of their piss
or a farm dog's call, distant
and near like an unborn child's.
Away from the tree, in the moon's country,
the fields are a lake.

And nothing disturbs you
there in the time before cities.
But at dawn, so the world can spin
and you can continue
on your path marked clear
between the power lines,
the horses and tree pretend again to be
just what they seem –
horses, a tree.

Glimpsed from a Moving Car

for Owen

Near Fridaythorpe
service station
on the A166

young woman
by the roadside
bent over a pram

ground-length hair on fire
as sunset shoots
through it

husband or boyfriend
smoking
gazing away.

Flood in the North

Walker,
tread carefully –
these days surfaces
are depths you can drown in.

Submarine under rain
that's changed its name,
the unlocked locks and weirs
have lost their purpose,
they've joined the workers
from the other redundant crafts
of old England, nation
of traded identities.

Look around you.
Feet out of sight, floating voters,
even the mallards have ducked
out of this cold coalition
of river and rain.

Hey, why not drink till we're sodden?
There's no such thing as *sobriety!*

And speaking of craft –
as usual, the pleasure-boats
are safe. See how they huddle
near the banks, hatches clenched,
smooth little arks
riding out the storm.

AND SHUTTLEWORTH

Inscribed in white brick on a former aircraft factory in Lincoln

for Ian Duhig

The mute mill signs its half-name to the sky,
can't help but ask what went before the AND, and who.
History may amputate, forget the facts, but these days
Dr Google proffers instant recollection. Call it snake oil,
but brick on brick the reconstructed answer lies in sepia
on a screen in the hands of the student of Creative Writing
workshop-walking by the Witham with tutor and peers.

CLAYTON, it turns out – clay now no doubt,
mortally uncoiled like his partner-in-capital
and those that made their names.
Around and about we sense the great braided river
of hours and, since we're all imaginative types, see
thinner than silk, thinner than air, a Sopwith Camel soar
over its half-demolished birthplace and our heads.

Up there the young pilot waves to us, backwards,
and high in his time perhaps foresees his end, or AND –
to land away along the towpath, now a bike-path,
Empire of convolvulus, cow parsley, autumn
wreckage, while swans settle in the shelter
of the ruined wall by the boat club, here
in the late English afternoon.

Plenty

In the mall entrance this rootless tree
lets the bloody rain
fall onto everything.

The carpark's monstrous appetite

   Mirage of the stacked shelves

       Slow landfill of the heart

As if the brand-new clothes
would burst through shop windows
multicoloured, screaming
for the missing children.

Democracy

Morning, before knowing, I watch the binmen in the raining street
scoop all the neighbourhood's carefully separated rubbish –
plastic / glass / paper – and cascade it into a wire-caged truck,
remixed, glorious, without difference,
in it together.

First to the radio – not *real* enough – so then to the reality of TV:
after all, *it's showtime for the truth*, folks, in dreaming America.
At the victory stage of victory he speaks softly, slowly, of healing,
at his back beautiful women and children, millionaires, racists,
and the roving eyes of bodyguards,

while here, ordinary morning unfolds. Coffee. Toast. Central heating.
Crowds of rain call from the drains with a muffled, sort of throttled
noise, and through the window the last flowers, *Coreopsis*,
bright as blackbird beaks in the grey air of England.

Now without warning I suffer the strange compulsion
to clean the whole house from top to bottom, to erase
what can most quickly be seen and named as waste,
dark stains, migrant dust, the ancient language
of spiderwebs, their fragile complexities,
and perhaps poetry, too – who needs it,
its demands, long memory,
nuance?

Poetry Train

i.m. Michael Donaghy (1954–2004)

Wonder how many of our fellow travellers
are reading poetry now on this train
O Donaghy, Donaghy? on laptops, phones
& tablets, maybe even, OMG, on paper,
while our adoptive England, yours and mine,
robust, dilapidated, glides by like a river in a 1950s documentary
now starring crap architecture, golf courses,
that dreaming Rupert Bear horizon of hills
over a scrapyard somewhere between Derby
and Doncaster while schoolkids cross a road
under a disused steeple, lone streetlight aglow in daytime
like a saint's halo.

Just me, yours, I'd guess, Michael,
who I can only know by this small book
where I look for better words after another
conference on Contemporary Culture in which disciples
bragged of their conversions, immersions, inversions,
and tweeted blindly.
Occasional tunnels snap the strands
of communion we talk and text in now,
journeying together but always somewhere else.

Yet what's no longer seen
still travels with us. Poetry
picks up where all the rest leave off
and at times arrives unannounced
like this train on this particular day, Michael,
that eased into the edges of an unknown town
a ragged nineteenth-century park late in the afternoon,
tall poplars raking the low sun to long shadows across the grass
and suddenly, no station in sight
stopped, all alight.

Riverside War Memorial

River has been where we are now
rose soft and passed like a sandman
spilling sand from his sleepless bed
leaves and limbs from upstream trees
naked to finger the winter winds.

River has been where we are now
knocked the wind from the marching reeds
swept the children's voices from their games
combed and caressed their green hair flat
left like a shadow with their names.

Fable

Fox, you have
no time for me,
looking for your life
in the world
at dusk.

Just a quick, cool
glance, at my stare,
then shift away,
shape slipping into all –
streets, regret, dark air.

Skin House

i.m. H. H. P.

*after Donald Rodney 'In the House of My Father';
photographic print on aluminium, 1997*

All the things your hands could do are done
and your handmade house, meticulous, is gone

a weathering stop homed in on a wave
no housing can withstand

but your sleeping house, so full of care
stands still in my dreaming hand.

*

Our skin is a house, and our house a skin
where we go to shelter our weathers in

thin-skinned in a street of passers-through
thin-skinned between the world and you.

Next

after Degas, 'Study of a Girl's Head', 1870s

Next he left the room
saying *You can go now*

so I did, put my own
clothes on and walked

back through the streets –
though not before peeking

at what he'd done,
sitting there, me

shoulders bare but
toasty, gazing out

all bright and thinking
of nothing special –

to my master's house
the grey old rooms
and fireplaces full of ash.

Lost Airmen, 1918

after a series of portraits by William Orpen

Young faces earth-borne
that now come only
to sleeping travellers
tossing restless
in roadside hotels
with bars, neon signs
and no thought of you.

Lullaby for a Baby Unborn in 1772, Written During the Neighbours' House Extension

after William Hunter, obstetrician, and Jan van Rymsdyck, artist,
'Anatomic drawing of a child in the womb in the 9th month of pregnancy'

O little man of lines,
I take the first of the day
to grieve for you in 1772,
though builders are changing
the world next door with hammers,
Radio 1, and one, at least,
singing loudly along.

There you lie
unsprung, afloat
in the articulate silence of ink,
ever ready to be born, forever
wasted on an upturned page
in the opened book of your mother's womb.

Yet this is art: to take time
to tell and not just mourn,
to lift things out of time
and hold them clear
as in the loving of curators,
to write, make marks, or sing.

Little one
in your paper boat,
artless you are art.
Things of beauty can't save us
but lend an unexpected caring.

(cont.)

So sleep on, no one,
never-to-be-one,
under glass in a room
in an old grave city.
With a hundred years of dust
the wall next door comes down
and sky re-enters, imparting.

Agostina Segatori in the Café du Tambourin

after Van Gogh

You seemed a long way from Earth, Agostina,
elbows on the gypsy music of that table
turning in the wild spring of Paris
your face struck by dreams
or was it mere regret?

What we settle for when life's burnt out
you said, inhaling, — *nothing but a cigarette*
someone else has smoked.
Yet on your head that joyous hat
and plume of red arisen flame

recalled as I went south
in an uncomfortable train
watching fields of sunflowers
pass dimly in the night.

PART TWO

Visitations

Wish

Blackbird caught
in the shed
while snow fell
all night

Let me open
the door for you
that familiar door
that holds things in

Fly into the white
air, vanish

Leave me just a trace –
ink on paper.

Not Visiting Madron

i.m. W. S. Graham (1918-86) and Nessie Dunsmuir (1909-99)

'Of course I saw in the distances the white speckles
of what are villages I'll never know'
– W. S. Graham letter to Ronnie Duncan, 9th Dec '78

Why are roads in Cornwall so crooked?
Because the road-builders kept their backs to the wind.
– Traditional Cornish saying

I

Picture it now: winter of '73 or '2, and we
knock on the door at Madron – Michael
or Arthur, Cathy, you or me. We've come over land
through the obstacles of distance and weather

(more easily done now most of us are gone)
along the phantoms of cart-width ways
where the high hedges blur as if in Google
or because we don't know quite where we're going

and are no longer there or here, for reading is time
without time, unanchored.

II

What colour, then, is the page of this day flapping
in landfall memory? Hilton blue or Hilton ochre,
Lanyon-red, moss-green Wynter, the deep amber wink
of whisky, or the jagged blues of the 'White Friends'?

All talk is translation, tapped here into addictive white,
Nicholson-white, the bone-white of polar knuckles
on Olympia portables, a trail of words I lay down now
like a road through the snow from Summerwell

to Madron, and us and you. Sorry to be so late.
I'd looked to come much sooner, but picks
rang over the fields, and the shiftless ghosts
of words kept turning their backs.

III

We knock again.
What tongues must we wander
to implement this encounter,
the distance and nearness
between writing and reading,
before and now?

What's true in the type-chatter?
Between the world and the head
the actual blows – or is it
just the language disturbed,
reading as best we can
in the falling light?

IV

And what's this place some like to be in,
writing while loved ones sleep in another room
or land, and the tired sun repaints the earth's far side?
You step out to star-watch or piss into the night, or listen
for the first curious bird of day.

This address admits light reluctantly, and we like that.
We try cities, but time and again are drawn back to edges,
the peripheries of flesh, sense, language, sea,
the world at arm's length, we trust,
for clearer seeing.

V

Now at the threshold
of the word-house
a woman in long love
appears, smiling, or does not.
She says: you're in and out.

She says: come back, look
into his dark room, but not
too deep into that gloom
which is there but
no longer here.

VI

Maybe next time you'll come over to ours?
We'll fetch you in the van, past Threebarrows
down that maze of tracks to the white door
by the egg factory.

We can be your children lost as the price of song.
From her vow of silence Cathy will serve a stew
of 'Layla', 'The Spiders from Mars', 'All the Young Dudes',
the new air's latest,

while Justin blows his horn by the tilting hedge
and seawind sifts three miles across the ordinary fields
from Agnes Head. Debbie and Norma will be there,
and our house-phantom Bal Maiden, *sans merci*,

and maybe one of them will sleep with you,
wrapped warm in patchouli or moorbreath,
your *langue* aged now in her mouth
but all your words escaping her.

VII

Now we're in a Greenock bar singing 'Who is Sylvia?'
Now we're writing the Lord's Prayer on a postage stamp
on a letter from Canada.
Now girls are laughing and foxes
are coming right up to us.
Now, Father, Mother, we fall
into Crete trailing words.
Now the perfect drugs have arrived
and we're maimed for the job.
Now we lay me down to sleep,
it's wind wet bracken noon in '44, '73, '86,
I'm heading for Scotland, you're heading
into night, having crossed all the distances.
Now it's time to go. Now it's then and then,
as usual, always and never.

VIII

I've looked for the place you were
close on fifty years. It will have been cold on the moor
from Summerwell to Madron, snow sheeted like paper
typed with stones, signs, black masts, all the obstacles
silent, gathered, strewn or sunk, the landing approximate.

But from their shifting sites the ghosts of words
have turned to face us.

On the tapped whiteness
we knock again.

Visitation

In bed, thickets
of summer night
and an odd scratching, very near –
creature of some sort?

Well, best give it a name
that sounds familiar,
'dog' or 'cat' or 'fox'...

Anyway, too late now –
it's right here beside you
smelling of cut weeds and rain.
You take the stern approach –

How did YOU get in?
Through the back door, as usual...

And, sure enough,
the door is wide open
and demonstrates this
by swinging slowly on its hinges

back and forth, back
and forth, and beyond it,
just out of sight,
the garden of childhood.

Pointless trying to sleep now.
No, just close the door, go back in
and enjoy this while it lasts –
father, mother, sisters, aunts, great-great uncles

even Scottish Granny on a visit from Toronto –
the whole family in their Sunday best
together again in the living room
as if nothing more had happened.

Arrival

for Hugh

Trickster, we're off-guard!
One whole moon ahead of plan
you spring your first joke –
two a.m., September night,
pulling the plug
in your private swimming pool.

*

In her old brown Hyundai Pony
Grandma gallops up
to see to your older brother.
She says: *I remember when…*
and in the street a boy
about fifteen
skates past us in the lamplight
with time on his hands.

*

Now your head comes free,
grey slick of vernix sewn
with blood, face averted, elfin ear
from another world,
and for the exact length of a breath
you're in two places at once
there and here, known and not –
another trick!

*

Then a hunched
shoulder, crazily small,
and quick as rain you're
with us and all the rest,
so utterly complete,
the first place gone
and only a thin rope of memory
trailing back from you.

*

Weeks later
beside our old house,
the autumn air was so still I heard
on the bare shingles
two storeys above me
a lone leaf land.

Return

Wake near a half-sunk
bruise-brown log
by a wide, still lake;
see that the wood
has human shape
and in fact is a boy
naked on his side
like a foetus half-unravelled,
face three-quarters
underwater,
eyes open. But
his skin pales now
and surprisingly soon
he's up and standing
before me, no longer
quite so helplessly beautiful
more like a grown son
and it's clear
he wants to share
the food, the remaining
plans, my walking
away from here
in my own footsteps,
with my breath, back
through the dark pines.

The Bargain

Made that summer afternoon,
crickets loud at the city's edge,
as we knelt in the cave you'd made
in your backyard by the drive-in
that screened the same white
silent movie all day.

In the dark of your den, pins
of sky leaked through like stars,
and the hot flattened floor was
crushed grass and milkweed
woven under our knees,
a carpet made of Canada.

It was a secret not to be told
to anyone, ever, and here
it was, little clown cyclops
peeping between the curtains
of your zipper. 'Your turn', you said.
But I'd seen the world now,
took the money and ran.

Hand

Her seat was next to an older man
and Annie said that on that long
bus-ride back down to Toronto
again and again his hand,
pretending sleep, crept
onto her thigh.

Annie was the loveliest, most distant
girl in school, too cool to laugh,
too cool to be, and as we walked
in the hot city nights guys called
from their passing cars
'Drop the boy – get a man!'

Annie moved away, I heard,
went west, had three children,
two boys, a girl, divorced.
With a smile she told me that beauty
was a darkness, a stranger's hand
waiting, not sleeping.

Sonnet on Distance

after Shakespeare's sonnet XLIV

I thought I knew I loved, and distances would prove it true.
That fall I jumped the sea alone, landed, but thought of you;
then, when you came, took lengths again to move away
and missed you, though thought it right we were apart!
Where my body was without, my thoughts were with you;
body with you, thoughts leapt the sea, or went
across miles to land's ends, knowingly.   This changed:
I came to think thoughts and flesh in one place should be,
returned, collapsed the thousand miles of thought to touch
your summer cheek, which turned its face away from me.
Not only land and sea, water, earth, time, but thought itself,
plays miles out in the space we let between our selves.
      What's distant can't be caught. I should have felt,
      and held, what far inside I'd known and thought.

———————

Sonnet XLIV, by William Shakespeare

If the dull substance of my flesh were thought,
Injurious distance should not stop my way;
For then, despite of space, I would be brought,
From limits far remote, where thou dost stay.
No matter then although my foot did stand
Upon the farthest earth remov'd from thee;
For nimble thought can jump both sea and land
As soon as think the place where he would be.
But ah, thought kills me that I am not thought,
To leap large lengths of miles when thou art gone.
But that, so much of earth and water wrought,
I must attend time's leisure with my moan,
            Receiving naught by elements so slow
            But heavy tears, badges of either's woe.

New Mother

The baby's head the shape of her mother's breast.
The baby's head in the street the size
of her mother's breast, the mother walking
in the street with the baby's head cupped
in her right hand between her breasts
under the high stone wall in the street
on the narrow path between the wall
and the speeding cars. The baby's head
in the sun in September between her breasts
like the sun itself cupped in her hand,
trees swimming overhead and the wave of late lavender
pouring from the wall onto her shoulder. The baby's head
between her breasts and the wave in the sun
and late bees in the lavender wall
and the fast, glinting cars.

A Woman in the Gatineau Hills Compares Her Recently Dead Husband to a Glacier

They keep a low profile,
these ground-down mountains.
Oldest in the world, he'd say,
so they've sure seen better days!
These days, polite, Canadian,
they barely bother the horizon
or press the sky away.

Is it strange to feel quickly ageless,
to recall a glacier's long goodbye
as though it was yesterday?
Slow mover, heavy partner
with time to spare,
calm on the surface
but a cruel undertow,
who left without warning,
slipped away dead north,
gouging in me scars
deep as lakes.

October now.
I gaze out of the car,
my son driving in the ice-clean light.
I feel the fall, all its leavings.
And the bears have come down close
to the city after a too-dry summer,
just mothers and their cubs,
here by the roadside
in these low, unhelpful hills,
hungry and searching.

Migrant

On Walmgate
by the River Foss,
before the Great War,
a German butcher, surname Angel,
prayed at St George's on Sundays,
sent his kids to Fishergate School,
served the locals with sausages and chops
and often dropped an extra trotter or two
into the baskets of the particularly poor,
some of whom, or someone else
(brother, son, father, uncle,
everyone knew who)
threw a brick, made in York,
through the shop window
one warm night
in August '14.

In the morning,
watched by children,
he sat weeping on the kerb,
wings nowhere
to be seen.

The Tallinn Swordsman

for John Greenwood

I met a modern swordsman in old Tallinn, who said
the past is passed through generations, in the blood –
wielding a blade for the first time, he claimed to know already
its weights and ways, its intimate link to ligament and air.

Now you and I wander this ancient Yorkshire village,
commuter dormitory, its green commons stopped up
with past pastiche. In the schoolyard by the churchyard
First Year children with toy bricks, barrows, spades,

build loudly in the sun, while among the graves
of bakers, farmers, the Towton dead, one small stone,
nestling shyly by the classroom wall, reads:
Mary Ann Boynton, Died 1947.

What was flows around us, old friend, as a river slips
over a flooded field watched by two young men long ago.

Little Shrines

In a plain Victorian terrace
thrown up for railway workers,
houses squeezed like brick soldiers
shoulder to shoulder,
in Romanesque alcoves
at shin-height

they guard the doors:
boot-scrapers, cast iron, elaborate.
At their apex, faces
the size of nineteenth-century pennies,
features blurred by muck and rust
to something between gargoyles and saints,

forgotten household gods
of the two-up two-down,
watched over the knackered drag
of boots tramping from the trainyards
up this narrow street clogged with strange,
unimagined cars.

The Green Councillor's Dream

In York the young ride bicycles
lightless at high speed, without bells
or whistles, the city's silent killers.
Just ask the Canada geese
as they squawk across the park,
unsanitary migrants no voting can displace.

In York the old ride bicycles too,
in helmets & day-glo,
with something like serenity,
peddling against twilit ambulances
with their underpaid staff
that will whisk them away
in the ancient Viking wind.

In York even the ghosts ride bicycles –
why, here comes William Etty, down from his fountain perch
on a paint-splattered two-wheeler, and nude (of course),
and there's Dicky Turpin,
hands behind his back and a broken neck,
Strictly done dancing on the old Knavesmire
while the tourists go *Oooooooooooh*…

In York the rivers in spate ride bicycles
of water through the streets and yards,
telling old tales under the pissing sky,
rain oiling their spoken wheels,
sanding the shores with leavings and goings.

York, flat as an aerodrome, perfect for cycling,
for recycling, for up-cycling! Soon everyone
will ride a bike and soon the cars will all be abandoned
rusting in the Park & Rides at the edges of the old city,
heaven recycled, cycle heaven.

Viking, Overheard

Next time I'll fuckin' kill him, she says,
decked top-to-toe circa 900 AD
and tossing a heavy horned
helmet into the ancient
plastic bin like a cabbage
or a certain man's
severed head.

Dregs of a long winter's day
among the festival tourists
and squalling half-term kids,
twilight sea-sky over the city roofs
on some of which the snow
from morning still lingers,
facing north.

Pink Magnolia

for Dianne

From its branch high above the street
a pigeon flaps like a wet towel
and glides across the liquorice-twisted stems
of iron railings planted by Victorian hands.

Legs white as birch saplings, a girl
in a green skirt and her mother pass by, pass,
and just beside them, near enough to touch,
the long black car slides by.

Now by the wall a man stops and stares.
Is he not quite all there?
Has he forgotten something, or remembered?
Or is it the sheer donated abandon
of all this pink flicked on the blue sky?

In a photograph by Humphrey Spender,
'Worktown, Bolton, 1937', a hearse goes by
over cobbles in the greyscale afternoon,
and everyone, each stranger, pauses
there in the street, removes his hat.

We should all wear hats,
even, if necessary, invisible ones
we can doff like mime artists on days like these
to mark a pigeon, a girl, a wondering man
while that black car goes by with all its wants
and magnolias flare in priceless air.

Prayer

Angel
look over our broken city.

Rise up if you can
though your wing is snapped

or climb down. Come
let's hitchhike over the borders

like we did when we were young
(though your thumbs may be missing).

Well OK, let's face it – neither of us
is going anywhere now.

But hey, it's spring again.
See the snowdrops finger up
through old Earth

and bright on their heels
the crazy, usual daffodils.

PART THREE

Riverain

The River Spoke

Kneel in me, said River,
let my countless
tongues lap you –
iber, wista, fleuve, رهن

Can't kneel, she said,
my legs are too stiff
from standing all day
on the warehouse floor.

Then lie in me, said River,
I'll take you on a cruise
in your dreams
beneath the stars…

Can't, he said,
my aged Mum, my noisy
kids, crave bread,
I must work.

Sleep then, forget. Here's a coin for your eyes,
dropped in old days by a king
in my darkness, plucked from the mud
of the common wealth…

We want to, but can't.
Invaders are coming, fire
is falling, fanatics call –
our neighbours need us.

Oh come, said River,
God's in his heaven, the walls
are strong, the bosses will provide.
You've earned your rest…

(cont.)

We won't, they said.
Your words are a flood of lies.
Though we've lost a lot,
it's too late to quit.

Then remain, said River,
I bless you. Take air,
gather, build, resist,
for as long as your flesh holds water.

Mutability

By the river
something is constantly
destroyed and re-made.

Distant over water,
the echo of a hammer,
the voice that says *change,*
while out of sight
the current swerves and hauls.

By the river
something is changing
ahead and in our wake,
here on the twin-track
of cause and effect

this green path running
along a poor small rise of earth
piled against Ouse.

Shoal

Swimming in wind, a shoal of sallow
leaves caught in light, sky fish
so bright they briefly blind
like spilled coins, silver
where the river
bends, loosens
its dark
purse.

River Walk

How quickly
the city falls away:
just past the last houses,
through a tall tree veil

a broad unforecast field
laid out in the sun like washing.
Above it, stacked clouds
survey the land, taking time
over distances;

and it seems we've stepped
into another place –
any green where
by a river in any time
in England –

as though, sleepwalking,
we've been awakened
or become children again,
horizons stretched with possibility.

Dilemma

for Jake Attree

Here beside us
the slow, clockless transit
of hours around these cattle,
patient in their pasture,
self-contained as planets.

But there, just
past the horizon,
the restless pull and hiss
of traffic on the bypass
Dopplers away west and east.

And we, men of a certain age
with our follies, skills, and scars,
on a path by a river
at the edge of an old city
caught on these horns,
two-timed.

Beneath the A64 Bypass Over the River Ouse

Highway invented in '76
(heatwave, ABBA's 'Dancing Queen')
thrown over river on two
long concrete hulls,
transaction in tonnage
between engineers and gravity
to save the city from passers-through;

and these eight pillars,
sad caryatids, staggered
to find themselves
in this Underworld
up to their waists
in thankless water
sunless earth

while over their heads
the thump and spray
of 70-mile-an-hour
B to A.

Marina

They sit, fat, sleek, shark-nosed in the sun
between the banks of their playground –
Susan, Bright Star, Wandering One.

Above them the oaks of summer sway
like sails, recall the time before engines,
this floating everywhere of leisure on display,

where lazy hulls slice river skin for fun,
make waves to finger its shores away.

Car Salesroom, River Foss

Sprung from dark woods and slipping away
old Foss, old before Domesday,

then made so filthy, so clogged with shit
you could almost, they say, walk on it.

Where muck sticks, brass will glow:
the factories come, but then they go.

Now walled, sequestered, forced askew,
a foreground for Mazda, Subaru.

River Being River

River being river passes
before we know it, in force
with a rush of the loosened and thrown,
or dull with a mask of everyday sameness,
its currents secret, subcutaneous.

Sky-fed, sewer, street, and field-fed,
seasoned with drink-cans and leaves
in the sun going down, or the thrash
of dawn rain on its skin,
river is past before we know it.

Punch Porteous Goes to the Races

On Saturday afternoon in summer 1930
at York Races Punch won a fortune, £17,
tramped back into town, bought a tin hip bath
and took it to the Red Lion where Uncle John's wife
Rose was publican and the boatmen-gypsies supped;
required of John to fill it full with drink, then
helped him and two others lurch it,
slopping on cobbles in the early evening light
to the tram stop, calling on all and sundry
Come take wine with me!
and cupping its contents for free
to drivers, passengers, passers-by,
(though in truth it was ale)
and the bath, once emptied,
by a drunken Punch
tossed into the Foss.

Gaze down from the bridge, they say,
in certain light, on certain days,
in the shallows, in the depths,
you can still see it among the vagrant
shopping carts, the swans.

November

Three days of rain over north
and by morning river, risen, crosses
the road to the rooted houses
like a great brown robe, nudging
before it an embroidered hem of leaves.

Surprised, the half-dressed trees
gaze down at their own reflections
cold water circling their feet
like a dream that doesn't stop
when you awake.

Ouse

River resuscitated, flesh
renewed by the rain's pummelling
acupuncture, stunned black and blue
and strewn with yellow leaves, slides away
under the hard-drinking trees.

Who stops to look?
The squirrel stock-still on a trunk;
the artist with his drowning box of tints;
the thin off-duty soldier, cursing the winter
and dreaming of Calabria.

And what's to see?
Bound up in its course
beneath the feeding rain
only river being river: a host of water
hauling the mortal weight of itself home.

On the Ings, After Rain

Eyes of water strewn
across the land

refugees gazing back
at their lost country.

Evening River

It's the hour of black birds
of light taking flight.

In the river the water is lucid yet secret,
its other sky holding fast to sunset.

And here's a moonful, O
so high over the willows and roofs
a round mouth stopped with opal

and sharing the glint of emptying slates
and the tilting bottle of these three young women
on the bench by the bank
that sleeves the river's endless departure.

A phone rings,
but muted, watery,
as though from yesterday.

All appears still
but is moving beneath.

The women and the willows
let their spring hair trail
in the leaving river,
the opal air.

Jenny

That Jenny was a one,
one of nine,
so with nine lives
strayed up and along
the narrow iron flange
of Scarborough bridge
swayed by one hand
high over the river,
pregnant with spring

rain. Shouted her ways
at the world, dared all
her sisters to follow,
married, had kids, slaved
thirty years in the chocolate works,
was gone.

Calls to us now
from the empty bridge –
waves, laughs, beckons.

Kingfisher

In deep shadow-shade
ever only half there –

then blue strobe,
gone, wish become air.

Diver

I dove from the bridge, scraped my knee
on the wall as I went. I saw where he'd gone
but river had shifted, tucked him away
to play with later. I went under once more,

found him asleep on his back
on his bed, the transparent sheets
unwrapping his beauty, forearm shielding
his eyes as though from the morning sun.

When I kissed him he stirred,
but it was only the wind of the water,
the current of time at his flesh,
not him awaking, not him awaking.

Riverain

Everywhere
water is finding itself.
In the earth, the streets,
it seeps and hammers,
strains to re-fuse its self
with its similar selves,
as if being alone is not enough.

Rain crowds down blue
through ambulance light, splinters
in pools where children's feet meet
their brief reflections,
rises fevered from forests,
branches away beneath cities
but always regathers.

Where water is broken
it mends, rebinds the torn,
resumes new shapes in mists, ditches,
cupped hands and bright ligaments
that draw sky towards sea over land,
each day accepting
all the mantles of pain and light.
We are compellingly water.

Acknowledgements

Some of these poems have previously appeared in *Acumen*, *The North*, *Pennine Platform*, *The Valley Press Anthology of Yorkshire Poetry* (Valley Press, 2017), and *A Small Box of River*, an artist's book with drawings by Jake Attree (2016). 'Sonnet on Distance' was published in *154* (Live Canon, 2016), in which 154 contemporary poets responded, one each, to Shakespeare's sonnets. A version of 'Sleeping Under a Tree Among Horses' was commended and published as part of the Troubadour Poetry Prize competition in 2015.

I'd like to thank Jake Attree for his engaging and inspiring company on a series of walks along the Ouse and Foss in 2015-16, the initial source of many of the river-themed poems in this collection. Lotte Inch Gallery, York, Salts Mill Gallery, Saltaire, and Woodend Media Centre, Scarborough, provided welcome support for *A Small Box of River*, both the artist's book and the exhibition.

Thanks go to York Museums Trust for commissioning me to lead a series of writing workshops in 2016-17 which resulted in 'Lost Airmen, 1918', 'Skin House', 'Next', and 'Lullaby for a Baby Unborn in 1772', all inspired by exhibitions at York Art Gallery. Thanks also to the Canal and River Trust 'Arts on the Waterways' programme for funding the film *The River Speaks*, co-produced with Ben Pugh, for which the poem 'The River Spoke' was written, and for co-funding a river walk and workshop with York Literature Festival in 2017, which also had help from The Poetry Society.

Fellow poets have contributed their advice on many of these poems. Ian Duhig encouraged me to write a poem inspired by W. S. Graham, and 'Not Visiting Madron' is the result. He, Lynne Green, and Ronnie Duncan provided information that helped with it. *Night Fisherman: Selected Letters of W. S. Graham* edited by Michael and Margaret Snow (Carcanet, 1999), and of course the Graham poems, were important sources.

My sincere thanks go also to Jamie McGarry and the team at Valley Press, and to Martha Sprackland for her intricate editing and thoughtful advice.

Notes

'Source', page 9

Rods and chains, theodolites, and zenith telescopes were all instruments used in surveying and precision mapping, most significantly for the *Anglo–French Survey* (1784–1790) and for the *Principle Triangulation of Great Britain* (1799–1853), the basis for the famous Ordnance Survey maps. Jesse Ramsden (1735–1800), born in Halifax, Yorkshire, was foremost among their manufacturers.

'   AND   SHUTTLEWORTH', page 16

Clayton & Shuttleworth, located at Stamp End in Lincoln, had a long history in engineering from 1842, embracing steam engines, threshing machines, tractors and, by World War I, aircraft, including the famous Sopwith Camel. I'm uncertain of the date when part-demolition of the mill resulted in the strange truncation of the company name, written large in white brick along the top of its river-facing frontage.

'Lullaby for a Baby Unborn in 1772, Written During the Neighbours' House Extension', page 25

The image that inspired this poem is *Engraving, Plate XIII,* in the book *Anatomia Uteri Humani Gravidi Tabulis Illustrata,* 1772. Poised between art and science, it was displayed as part of the exhibition 'Flesh' at York Art Gallery in 2016-17.

'Not Visiting Madron', page 32

From 1967 the poet W. S. Graham (1918–1986) lived with his wife Nessie Dunsmuir in a terraced cottage in Madron, Cornwall. They were friends with many of the artists associated with St Ives, hence the references. The 'White Friends' are amphetamines, specifically Benzedrine. 'Bal' is Cornish for mine, and a 'bal maiden' was a term used in the eighteenth and nineteenth centuries for a young woman working in the mining industry.

'Woman in the Gatineau Hills Compares Her Recently Dead Husband to a Glacier', page 45

The Gatineau Hills are an ancient part of the Canadian Shield mountain range and form the north side of the Ottawa Valley, on the Quebec side. I grew up looking at them across the Ottawa River.

'The River Spoke', page 55

رهن, pronounced 'nahr', is the Arabic word for river.